CONSCIOUS
DEVELOPMENT

CONSCIOUS DEVELOPMENT

ANOTHER APPROACH TO SUSTAINABLE DEVELOPMENT

Gutu Kia Zimi, PhD

authorHOUSE®

AuthorHouse™ LLC
1663 Liberty Drive
Bloomington, IN 47403
www.authorhouse.com
Phone: 1-800-839-8640

Published by AuthorHouse 05/02/2014

ISBN: 978-1-4969-1070-7 (sc)
ISBN: 978-1-4969-1071-4 (e)

Any people depicted in stock imagery provided by Thinkstock are models,
and such images are being used for illustrative purposes only.
Certain stock imagery © Thinkstock.

This book is printed on acid-free paper.

Because of the dynamic nature of the Internet, any web addresses or links contained in
this book may have changed since publication and may no longer be valid. The views
expressed in this work are solely those of the author and do not necessarily reflect the
views of the publisher, and the publisher hereby disclaims any responsibility for them.

Contents

DEDICATION

To
Shirley
Paul Gutu Kia Zimi
Jeffrey Gutu Kia Zimi
My inspiration

The truth that makes men free is for the most part
the truth which men prefer not to hear
Herber Agar

Powerful nations rise and fall,
brave men and women give their lives to a noble cause,
but ideas can last forever

PREFACE

This book is an inquiry into an area that is timely and important for the promotion of human society: Development. It offers a new concept on which we can debate: conscious development. What is it? What is the main difference between the new concept of conscious development and the concepts used to refer to development so far by all the actors involved in the process of development or human development? In other words, what is original in the new concept I proposed hereby? It is there that reside the courage and merit of the author. Indeed, in this book, the author first briefly reviews and discusses the different concepts of development, the most widespread and popular include: development as economic growth, community development, integrated and comprehensive development, endogenous development, self-reliant development, integrated rural development, sustainable development, eco-development, human development, etc. The author tries to demonstrate that each concept of development is related to actual facts that have characterized the communities' historical development. He gives for each concept the context that lead to its elaboration. Endogenous development for example advocates the idea of a kind of development that has an internal origin, development of which the impulse sterns from within a society; sustainable development supposes a kind of development that reflects the current concerns and those of future generations, eco-development is conducive to development that makes use of local knowledge and solutions to solve local problems, integral development reflects the Christian view of development which targets the development of every man and all individual. The current development concepts focus on economy, technology and scientific knowledge to achieve the community overall welfare. But, it is becoming increasingly clear that the serious current problems of humanity are not scientific or technological, but rather moral, because if they were scientific or technologic, we could have already resolve them as Loron Wade states: *So why do we still have hunger, violence, tyranny, because the worst problems of the age are not scientific but moral problems. If they were scientific or technological problems, we would have solved them long ago* (Wade Loron, 2006).

Similarly, as pointed out by Pope John Paul II: *"The evil is not in the"* assets *"as such but in the fact of getting these assets in a way that meets neither the quality nor the value order of these assets, quality and value order that arise from the subordination of goods and making them available at the welfare, of man and his true vocation. The exclusive pursuit of "having" is therefore an obstacle to man's growth and opposes his true value. "(« Le mal ne constitue pas dans l' « avoir » en tant que tel mais dans le fait de posséder d'une façon qui ne respecte pas la qualité ni l'ordre des valeurs des biens que l'on a, qualité et ordre des valeurs qui découlent de la subordination des biens et de leur mise à la disposition de l' « être» de l'homme et de sa vraie vocation. La recherche exclusive de l'« avoir» fait dès lors obstacle à la croissance de l'être et s'oppose à sa véritable grandeur »*(Pope John Paul II, Encyclical Letter Sollicitudo Rei Socialis). Rolon Wade and Pope John Paul II's claims stress the moral and ethical dimension of development. This is where the concept of conscious development complements the other concepts formerly developed and finds its originality. For the author, conscious development, far from being an intellectual utopia, would reconcile the physical (growth), spiritual, cultural, social, moral, ethical aspects of development in the perspective and purpose of development characterized not only by the economic aspect of growth and the acquisition of material goods, but also by the moral, spiritual, cultural, social and ethical aspects as pointed out by Donella Aurelio Pecci: « Never failed to conclude that

the answers to the world's problems begin with a new humanism »
(Donella, M.et all., 2004). Conscious development aims at meeting
Hirschman's paradigm which states: « *At the end it will be possible to
see a kind of social science that would be very different from what most of
us have practiced ; a moral-social science where moral considerations . . .
will no longer need to be smuggled or be unconsciously expressed, but may
be exposed overtly and innovertly. This is in fact the social science that I
dream for our grandchildren* » (« *Au bout du chemin il sera alors possible
d'apercevoir une sorte de science sociale qui serait très différente de celle que
la plupart d'entre nous ont pratiquée; une science moralo-sociale . . . où les
considérations morales n'auront plus besoin d'être introduites en fraude ni
d'être exprimées inconsciemment, mais pourront être exposées ouvertement
et innocemment. Voici en tout cas la science sociale dont je rêve pour nos
petits-enfants* » (Hirschman, quoted by Elsa Assidon).

The development new concept is based on what Maharishi
Mahesh says: « *The determining factor in quality life in society, is the
level of coherence or integration of the collective consciouness* » (« *Le
facteur déterminant de la qualité de la vie dans la société, c'est le niveau
de cohérence ou d'intégration de la conscience collective* » *(Maharishi
Mahesh Yogi)*. For the author, conscious development is essentially
characterized by its comprehensiveness, since it includes all the
features of the other development concepts discussed, emphasizing
the fact that any development, to be community wide, total and
integrated, endogenous, sustainable, human, etc., it must above all be
conscious, because it is consciousness, and consciousness alone, which
would allow the realization of the objectives pursued by the different
communities. The concept of conscious development is opposed to
the current development model based on growth performance and
economic liberalism, caring very little about the level of resources and
their exhaustion. This desire to acquire as much property as possible,

sometimes without moderation, is the basis of adverse consequences that characterize today's human and: acute poverty, minorities interest contempt, resource overexploitation, environmental degradation, conflicts of interest, contempt for universal values, economic and military domination, etc. For the concept of conscious development, the development objective of a company is to provide its members with a better quality of life, that is to satisfy the individuals and community needs while ensuring the sustainability of the society and setting up structures and corresponding means to achieve this goal. Development must be a conscious act, because development without conscience ruins communities. The peculiarity of the proposed new concept lies in the fact that consciousness is a factor of growth and development. Indeed, consciousness awareness in the production can but contribute to growth and economic development, as well as to a better distribution of this growth within the community. Individual and collective awareness needs to be the basis to development issues solutions in the community. The collective consciousness of a community is, indeed, the entire group consciousness. Maharishi asserts that « *the fundamental force that governs the quality of social life is the collective conscience of society* » (« *la force fondamentale qui gouverne la qualité de la vie sociale est la conscience collective de la société* » (Maharashi Mahesh Yogi).

The concept of conscious development is primarily a conscious process of imagination characterized by conscious acts in response to various community problems through educational action following a "socio" logic. The concept of conscious development is to respond to this statement from Herbert Agar: « *The truth that makes men free is for the most part the truth which men prefer not to hear* » (Herbert Agar quoted par David Icke, 2003). The concept of conscious development, according to the author, must lead to "a revolution of consciousness" which is as fundamental as were the revolutions of science, industry and technology have been (Theodore Monod). This vision of a revolution in consciousness is a specificity and all the aspects referred to above constitute the originality of the proposed concept. We must be courageous to do it, and the author dares launch a new concept, being aware that in the jungle of science and ideas, this is not to be immediately accepted. Its great merit is to have dared.

Dr Félicien Lukoki Luyeye
Professor Emeritus
University of Kinshasa
Catholic University of Congo

CHAPTER I

INTRODUCTION

Development models previously accepted and supported by the authors from developed countries are now heavily criticized both in these countries as well as in developing countries. In the late 1960s, already theories of development based on the equation Growth= Development equation on the one hand, as synchronic stability, that is to say at a specified moment (such as classical and neo-classical and postkeynésien models) and, on the other hand, as a diachronic stability, that is to say according to the evolution in time (such as historical school, growth patterns, and the Marxist model) led to an impasse. A number of fundamental premises questioning the "what were the causes and factors of this economic growth" have not stood the test of experience, whether those concerning the essence and nature of development or those on the internal and external conditions of development as well as the objectives and the means for establishing these conditions. These development models have privileged more the material and financial aspect of development, characterized primarily by profitability, the social aspect in its human values. Until recently, structural adjustment programs advocated by the International Monetary Fund (IMF) lined up on this logical priority of economic growth by applying the so-called performance criteria, which actually asphyxiate the economies of the developing countries. It is worth reminding here that required the implementation of corrective action by implementing Adjustment Social Dimension programs (SDA) and more recently by the development of strategy documents on poverty reduction. These development models

1

are an obstacle to community development because on the one hand, they do not allow a socio-economic integration of the latter, and on the other hand, they mainly contribute to their economic marginalization.

In this regard, Etienne Ndongala Tadi Lewa argues that modern economic systems have many obstacles to the integration of traditional societies; while Samir Amin suggests the dominance of the capitalist mode of production as the dominant world system, organized, hierarchical, that dominates all the other modes of production under its sphere and subjects them to its own laws. The development model advocated and supported worldwide is one that relies primarily on economic performance defined in terms of growth or economic development. This design promotes the development and breeds poverty, which is today one of the greatest threats to the future of the planet, since the accumulated wealth is the basis of gross inequalities and other conflicts, since it is not beneficial to most communities. EE Hagen asserts moreover that in reality, economic growth may make poor families become even poorer. It goes without saying that this model favors the accumulation of more wealth (material goods) to the detriment of man and his environment, especially his moral and social values, human and spiritual. This development model, which has its basis in the economic growth, also promotes the development of a consumer society to the detriment of the level of resources and the environment. This requires the reorientation of growth and welfare in developing countries, that is to say that « *we must promote both growth and further growth*». (*Il nous faut promouvoir à la fois une croissance et une autre croissance* (J.M.Albertini). This implies then profound changes and adaptations of these economics because they disrupt the stability of the environment, thereby undermining the survival of man. It is clear that the different theories and models of development that have characterized the successive decades of development have demonstrated their weaknesses regarding the limits of natural resources. The first report of the Club of Rome issued a severe warning that: *« If the world continues in spite of all the warnings to produce and consume increasingly, production and consumption will eventually stop under the pressure of irrestible forces and will bring bankruptcy the system»* (*« Si l'humanité continue malgré tout à produire et à consommer de façon croissante, la production et la consommation devront un jour cesser sous la pression des forces désormais incontrôlables et amèneront la faillite du système* (C.Furtado»).

According the WWF report, *"human demands on the planet exceed supply. Humanity's ecological footprint exceeded the earth's biocapacity by more than 50% in 2008. In recent decades the carbon footprint is a significant component of this ecological overshoot. Biocapacity per person decreased from 3,2 global hectares (gha) in 1961 to 1,8 gha per capita in 2008, even though total global biocapacity increased over this time. Rising consumption trends in high-income groups around the world and BRIICS countries, combines with growing population numbers, provide warning signs of the potential for even larger footprints in the future"*[1]. This situation urges us to think and rethink the concept of development currently in use. The myth of growth, whatever it is, still has, at any price, a seductive power in our minds. The rejection of the idea of growth for growth leads us to a future that would allow us to guide our thinking and to envision a new type of development, conscious development and concerned with our future and our resources. The question is not what the volume growth should be, but what kind of growth to fight

---

[1]   WWF, Living Planet Report 2012, www.wwf.org., p.12.

for. In this connection, the Vézelay's[2] states clearly: « *For the first time in history, human activity is running the risk of irreversibly altering the fundamental balance, necessary to life on our planet*»[3] (« *Pour la première fois dans l'histoire, l'activité humaine risque d'altérer de façon irréversible les équilibres fondamentaux nécessaires à la vie de notre planète* »). In this mess and looting of the natural heritage of mankind, the northern hemisphere, J.Ki-Zerbo states, is undoubtedly the prime contractor. First, because it takes by far more than its share of these limited resources. And secondly, because, by its very model of production and consumption, it pushes all the world people to saw the branch on which they are installed. In fact, peoples are losing the reason to make a choice between good and bad, and the conscious to do right activities to promote the welfare of the community. Consequently, an imbalance is observed, firstly, on the objective of development, that of promoting the material, social, moral and spiritual welfare of their communities and, secondly, on the resources and environment. We must confront this situation before it's too late.

Despite the failure of the development models in use and the fears for the future, many people think that the economic growth has already come across some constraints and various historical obstacles on its upward path and that the risks are an integral part of this route, as that is the price to pay to stay in the train of progress. Unfortunately, we

---

[2]   Le groupe de Vézelay, qui a lancé cet appel, est composé de huit membres (originaires de trois continents) dont : Calliope et Michel Beaud, Mohamed Larbi Bougherra, Pierre Calame, Venant Cauchy, Maurice Cosandey, Joseph Ki-Zerbo et René Loubert. Constitué en 1986 avec l'appui de la Fondation pour le Progrès de l'homme (FPH), ce Groupe s'efforce de créer les conditions d'une réflexion permanente et globale sur l'homme, l'humanité, le monde et leur devenir.

[3]   J. KI-ZERBO, Compagnons du Soleil. Anthologie des grands textes de l'humanité sur les rapports entre l'homme et la nature, Unesco/La Découverte, Ed. Charles Léopold Mayer (FPH), Paris, 1992, p.7.

quickly and often forget that the nature of risk has changed and today the main concern is man's survival. It is important to note that is no growth without existence. But the current development, considering only the aspect of economic growth, threatens the true existence and survival of man. It is also true that progress, seen under the current development model, is the matter of a few in a very short term, while the potential risks of accidents, may be irreversible and affect all living beings[4]. From the foregoing perspective, conscious development that we support is a necessity, because it offers a new development direction. For example, it is difficult today to assess the exact cost of deforestation in economic terms, but this cost is certainly a very high cost. Paul W. Richards wrote, «. . . *that much of the animal and plant life in the tropics may disappear before we have started to study it*» («. . . *qu'une grande partie de la vie animale et végétale des tropiques peut s'éteindre avant même que nous ayons commencé à l'étudier* ») well «. . . *an immense field of human potential can disappear without leaving any evidence.*» («. . . *qu'un immense domaine de potentialités humaines peut disparaître sans laisser le moindre témoignage* »). M.L. Bouguerra on his behalf says, « *Every environmental threat takes two decades for people to be aware and organized, another decade to undertake any preventive measures*»[5] (« *Chaque menace environnementale prend deux décennies pour que les gens se mettent en colère et s'organisent, une décennie supplémentaire pour que des mesures de prévention quelconques soient prises* ») and it will take another decade to witness the application of decision. According to Ervin Laszlo, « *Biodiversity loss is the other long-term threat to human survival . . . current human activity is shredding this fabric of life. Before*

---

[4]   J. KI-ZERBO, op.cit., p.7.

[5]   M. L. BOUGUERRA, La pollution invisible, UPF, Paris, 1997, p.7.

humans appeared on the planet, the rate of species extinction was about one per million per year, about the same rate as new species came into existence.

Today, human activity has upped the rate of extinction to about 1000 per million per year »[6] *(La perte de la biodiversité est une autre menace à long terme à la survie de l'humanité . . . les activités humaines courantes sont en train de détruire cette source de vie. Avant que l'homme n'apparaisse sur la planète, le taux d'extinction d'espèces était de un par million par an, c'est le même taux pour les nouvelles espèces qui apparaissaient. De nos jours, les activités humaines ont augmenté le taux d'extinction d'espèces à 1.000 par million par an).* According to the WWF, *"biodiversity has declined globally; the global living planet index declined by almost 30 % between 1970 and 2008; the global tropical index declined by 60% during the same period; the global temperate index increased by 31%; however this disguises huge historical losses prior to 1970; the global terrestrial, freshwater and marine indices all declined, with the freshwater index declining the most, by 37%; the tropical freshwater index declined even more precipitously, by 70%"*[7]. Many organizations, scientists and researchers have described and explained, with the support of accurate statistics, the nature and pace of the processes that undermine the basic metabolism of our land[8]. Among other causes of environmental impacts, mention can be made of the operation of the consumer society, which involves the exploitation and transformation of low entropy resources into goods and services of all kinds and sources of energy necessary to meet human needs. The ultimate outcome of these environmental impacts are manifested through lots of liquid, solid, gas and radiation releases. These effluents, sometimes severely toxic, modify the various receiving

---

[6]   E. LASZLO and P. SEIDEL: Global Survival: The Challenge and its Implications for Thinking, Selectbooks Inc, USA, 2006, p.184.

[7]   WWF, Living Planet Report 2012, in www.wwf.org, op.cit., p.12.

[8]   J. KI-ZERBO, op.cit, p.7.

environments, with consequent environmental problems such as water, soil and air pollution, trophic chains contamination, acid rain, global warming, destruction of the ozone layer, ecological balance disrupts, etc., Mohamed Larbi Bouguerra asserts that, our planet, continues to serve as a receptacle to countless chemicals and wastes. It is even said that every day, our planet becomes more toxic with more than four million chemicals are now circulating among people.

Moreover, a study of the National Center of Economic Studies in Washington, based on 21 indications of environmental trend in nine industrialized countries, says that the quality of the environmental has deteriorated considerably during the last twenty years. [9] (Notre planète ne cesse de servir de réceptacle à d'innombrables produits et déchets chimiques. On va même jusqu'à dire que, de jour en jour, notre planète devient plus toxique puisque plus de quatre millions de produits chimiques circulent aujourd'hui entre les hommes. D'autre part, une étude du Centre National d'Etudes Economiques de Washington, se fondant sur 21 indicateurs de tendance environnementale dans neuf pays industrialisés, affirme que la qualité de l'environnement s'est considérablement dégradée au cours de vingt dernières années). For Anthony McMichael[10], « *the human race faces a new threat to his health and perhaps even to his survival*».[11] (« *la race humaine fait face à une nouvelle menace pour sa santé et peut-être même pour sa survie* »). For Ulrich Beck quoted by ML Bouguerra, *we have come into reality in a "risk society", which forced to fight the battle against two enemies: an outside enemy, and against an "inside" enemy technology and organization*»[12]

---

[9]   M. L. BOUGUERRA, op. cit., p.13.

[10]   Président du Comité de santé environnementale du gouvernement australien.

[11]   J. Bartlett, Are We Really Safe as Houses? The Guardian, 3 déc.1996, cité par M.L.BOUGUERRA, op. cit. p.6.

[12]   Cité par M.L. BOUGUERRA, ibid., p.9.

(nous entrons en réalité dans « la société du risque », qui contraint à livrer le combat à la fois contre l'ennemi extérieur de la nature et contre l'ennemi « intérieur » de la technique et de l'organisation.). In fact, the problems posed by toxic substances in our environment are closely linked to lifestyle and contemporary economies. These issues challenge scientists and the agenda a re-evaluation of production and consumption and why not investment modes. They also require an analysis of the solutions proposed to restructure the economy and decision making to move from a situation ignoring or paying little attention to environmental realities with a new approach to the relationship between economic activity, men and the various compartments of the ecosystem[13]. In addition to this impact category, there are concomitant environmental penalties, which have their origin, not anymore, in industrialized countries, but in developing countries. They are the consequence not anymore of the mass consumption, but of the underdevelopment, of the poor development and poverty. Many environmental problems are rooted in people's poverty developing countries, forced, to ensure their immediate survival needs, to use inappropriate resources on their lands.

This misuse leads, consequently, to a procession of serious environmental damages[14]. At the United Nations Conference on the Human Environment Conference in Stockholm in 1972, Indira Gandhi, then Prime Minister of India, said: *« How can we ask those who live in villages and slums to preserve the purity of air, rivers and oceans when their own lives are flawed? Don't think the misery of the poor and the greed of the rich are the most serious nuisance? (« Comment peut-on demander à ceux qui vivent dans les villages et les bidonvilles de préserver la pureté de l'air, des rivières et des océans quand leur propre vie est viciée?*

---

13   M.L. BOUGUERRA, op. cit., p.11.

14   D. M. KABALA. op. cit. p. 51.

La misère des pauvres et l'avidité des riches ne sont-elles pas les nuisances les plus graves? »).

Sound management of the environment and natural resources is now considered a prerequisite, but not as an obstacle to development and is a key element of any program to improve the living conditions of populations. The resources in question here are not only those of the soil and subsoil, but also those of a primitive now limited nature on our planet ravaged by the progress of the modern industrialized world, streamlined, standardized and on which depends the survival of our species, because nothing can replace nature. The World Charter for Nature goes further by proclaiming that *"(. . .) any form of life is unique, warranting respect regardless of its usefulness to man."* The analysis of environmental problems, their understanding and the finding solutions involve that the environment and development be treated in a global perspective, as two interdependent sets. In other words, the long-term improvement of the quality of the global environment must go with the development of communities on the one hand, and on the other hand, by a shift, in the rich countries, of the consumption habits. Poor countries are also concerned because they must also reorient their way of consuming and especially to organize themselves to produce what they consume. This is a new approach to development as proposed by conscious development and development monad model. The growth patterns of developing countries and industrialized countries must become human sustainable development models, but to do so, they must be replaced by a development model more concerned with the formation of mankind consciousness and his future for a better management, at all levels, of the resources and the environment according to the proposed development conscious approach.

Moreover, industrialized countries can afford to slow down an energy-intensive material growth while improving the welfare of their populations. We often forget that the cost of catching up living standards, if they remain focused on material consumption, would be unbearable. These countries need, in order to make up, adopt new techniques and comprehensive policies to limit the pressure exerted on the capacity of the planet. It is for these countries to promote a new direction of development according the concept of conscious development. To this end, we can refer to this African proverb: « *Money is good, but man is better, because he responds when spoken to*» (« *L'argent est bon, mais l'homme est meilleur, parce qu'il répond quand on lui parle* »).

As be seen, economic growth is good but it does not automatically improve community welfare; the balance of resources is necessary because it ensures the basic needs and communities aspirations. In response to this concern, we consider that the best way to achieve the improvement of communities living conditions and the balance between growth and resources is promoting a conscious development underpinned by the monad development model. This is more necessary than ever since each decade brings new challenges. Today, half of the world population has less than two dollars a day to live, 80% of people worldwide share 20% of the global GDP and in each country, there is a big gap between rich and poor and this not all . . . [15]. In 2005, according a report in Time Magazine, "nearly 30% of Britain's annual income went to the top 5% earners. Meanwhile, more than 33% of American income goes to the top 5% of earners. Worldwide, about 1,4 billion people live on $1,25 (US) or less a day, and 25,000 children die daily because of poverty". At the African continental level, the analysis of the economic situation and development state demonstrate that the random path followed so far and that is to let things go, has led to disasters in Africa. The continent potential in terms of natural resources, has seriously eroded and the people's living conditions display a serious

---

[15] J. D. WOLFENSOHN, Les défis de la mondialisation. Le rôle de la Banque Mondiale, Banque Mondiale, Paris, 2001, p.4.

stagnation or even regression. Despite the large number of strategies and action plans and recommendations, no substantial progress has been. On the contrary, the situation has worsened and continues to worsen.

Moreover, there appears to be no consensus on the ways or patterns of development to follow, and especially which approach should govern the recovery of the situation in the continent. Conscious development and the monad development model we support offer a new approach to development and environment issues to get the consensus that is expected to address the situation in Africa. This is necessary because opportunism, inexperience and inappropriate knowledge of the concept of development block the search of consistent solutions to the situation in which our continent is. Our observations also show that our communities often overuse, to the satisfaction of their needs, their available natural resources. They degrade their environment and live poorly because they are not able to do otherwise. These attitudes are often the result of political and economic context, consequence of aggregate errors of development policy. Experience shows that not only the industrialized countries impose, on developing countries, development models that match their interests, but also that in developing countries, political leaders adopt development models that do not always meet the needs and aspirations of their communities. In the case of our continent, Africa is like the slave laboratory on which all tests are carried out to see which ones are successful. Unfortunately for Africa, these tests are more failures than successes. Left unattended, people are in search of life and survival strategies to get rid of their planned misery. Unfortunately, these strategies often disconnected from national policies do create in most cases but disappointment[16]. It is in

---

[16]   F. LUKOKI LUYEYE, Vivre et survivre à Kinshasa. Problématique du développement humain, Collection Afrique et Développement 19, FED/FCK, 2004, p.8.

this context that J.Kizerbo recommends: « *It is important to undertake mental process first, later a collective one, then say: I am the center of myself. As Africans say, we can not shave someone in his absence. This means that no one can take my peace, unless I surrender*». (« *Il faut réaliser une opération mentale individuelle d'abord, collective ensuite, et se dire: je suis le centre de moi-même. Comme disent les africains ; on ne peut pas coiffer quelqu'un en son absence. Ceci veut dire que personne ne peut se substituer à moi-même, sauf si je me laisse faire* »). For over 50 years, donors from the West have replaced Africans to think and plan their development.

According to an African proverb: « *Whoever sleeps on someone other's mat should considers himself as sleeping on the ground*» (« *Quiconque dort sur la natte d'autrui doit se considérer comme dormant à terre* ») to the extent that the owner of the mat at any time may withdraw his mat. We must be the center of ourselves rather than the periphery of another person's center[17]. According Issaka Herman Traoré, Africa has entrusted its development in others, particularly in the West. All theories of development experienced in Africa come from outside, especially from the West. Aren't there any African development thinkers? Aren't there any, social sciences in Africa? Why then, do not the latter produce endogenous theories that reflect the aspirations and realities of African people so that those African people use them to increase their livelihoods for better living conditions. The reason is twofold: the brainwashing to which Africans have been subjected for centuries has given rise to an inferiority complex. This complex occurs separately in the depth of the African soul, but also and especially by the rejection of everything that is produced by an African. Others feel that this production cannot be good, because from within. Today, African intellectuals even when they are convinced that the concepts of relooks, of the donors are "du déjà vus et connus", prefer to follow the process, instead

---

[17]   J. KI-ZERBO, op.cit., p.183.

of producing alternative theories and evidence that could demolish some theories. The few intellectuals who venture in this way are administratively, professionally, economically, academically muzzled, as was the case of Cheikh Anta Diop, Kwame Nkrumah with the pan-Africanism, Negritude with Senghor, Mobutu with the policy of the authenticity, Ki-Zerbo, etc. Whose theories have never gone beyond the circles of some African elite, in contrast to their contemporaries in Latin America, such as Paulo Freire and his theory of consciousness that has paid off or Escobar with his dependency and development deconstruction theory[18]. Each of these African proposed alternatives that could take Africa out of its eternal state of lethargy, but because they were isolated, they were overcome by imperialism and neo-colonialism. These development theories from donors were in general inappropriate to the mainland, or better they only helped to better subjugate Africans, to better exploit them, while at the same time refusing to consider African alternatives to their pompous and misleading theories. These theories of development have brought only misery, desolation and acculturation to the continent[19].

According to Nzanda Buana, the Sub Saharan African countries are dragged behind compared to other world nations. This delay is explained by the fact that theories applied in Black Africa an inappropriate. Hence the necessity to invent a new way of theorizing African economies and apply really progressive strategies[20]. Anyway, why do Africans themselves

---

[18] I. H.TRAORE, les alternatives africaines aux théories de développement des bailleurs de fonds, www.etrangerencontre.org, p.9.

[19] I. H.TRAORE, op.cit., p.11.

[20] M. NZANDA BUANA, L'économie politique de l'Afrique Subsaharienne. Approche historique et théorique. Thèse de doctorat en économie, Faculté des Sciences Economiques, Université de Kinshasa, Septembre 2007, cité par A. TSHIAMBI in « M. NZANDA BUANA préconise l'adaptation des théories économiques aux réalités africaines, www.lepotentiel.com/afficher_article.php, édition 4185 du 23 novembre 2007.

continue to remain in this permanent state fetal instead of refusing this subjection? The answer lies in education and the awakening of communities consciousness as suggested in the conscious development. It is therefore necessary to promote men aware of the conditions of this own development as suggested by the conscious development and monad development model. From the foregoing, Conscious development is an essential element in community development. We argue that if the different development models considered so far have not yielded the desired results, it is because the vision of development was more focused on economic growth and profitability than to consciousness growth in the development process. Creating a man conscious of his own development remains the primary objective of conscious development. It could take a long procedure but as Dr Martin Luther King Jr said: "time is always right to do what is right."

Chapter II

CONCEPTS OF DEVELOPMENT

2.1. EVOLUTION OF THE CONCEPTS OF DEVELOPMENT

When one examines how development issues have been addressed, one should note that the evolution of ideas was very dynamic and punctuated by some historical, political, socio-economic and technological facts. In terms of thought, it is important to observe that there have been both opening, diversification and convergence and sometimes divergence of ideas. This led to the evolution of different development concepts such as community development, integrated development, integrated rural development, endogenous development, harmonized development, unified development, global development, uneven development, basic development, local development, balanced development, self-development, self-centered and self-confident development, sustainable development, human development, and eco-development.

Whatever the concept, there is something obvious: development is a very complex reality, which varies and charges according to the vagaries of historical and political facts and according to different factors and constraints that accompany it. A certain fact emerges from the foregoing: development is complex but not chaotic. The factors that underlie the emergence of these new ideas or new directions of development are different, they are historical, economic, technological and scientific, religious, political, social, environmental, etc. Hence there is need for a constant and gradual adaptation of the theory and ideas about development dependent on times and circumstances considered. The emergence of new concepts on development is also favored by the reality of facts. This led Samir Amin to state that, « *Development has broken down it theory is in a deep crisis, its ideology, the subject to doubt*» (« *Le développement est en panne, sa théorie en crise, son idéologie, l'objet de doute* »).

According to Iraida Aleshina, the emergence of new concepts is linked to the crisis of old conceptions, that guided the debate on underdevelopment, a crisis that had become quite obvious during the second United Nations decade on development[21]. Indeed, according to Mbaya Mudimba, « (. . .) *for more a third than century, formulas such as "self-centered development" "integrated development", "development at the root" and "community development" have been applied on for their development developing countries whether supported by political options or ideologies of government regime in power in the country, by northern countries, or by companies or organizations created for this purpose, these approaches have often failed. This failure is mainly due to the difference between the concept of development within the populations affected by the development and that of the proponents often oriented by the action of transnational capital and hidden of the latter*»[22] («(. . .) *pendant un tiers de siècle, les pays du Sud se sont vus appliqués des formules comme celles du "développement auto-centré", du "développement intégré", du "développement à la base" et du "développement communautaire", pour leur développement. Qu'elles aient été soutenues par des options ou idéologies politiques du régime gouvernemental au pouvoir dans le pays, par des pays*

---

[21] I. ALECHINA, The Contributing of United Nations Systems to Formulating Development Concepts, in Different Theories and Practices of development, Unesco, Paris, 1982 citée par O. P. SANTOS, op.cit., p.224.

[22] R. M. MBAYA, op. cit. p. 8.

du Nord, ou par des sociétés ou organismes créés à cet effet, ces différentes formules ont souvent échoué. Cet échec est essentiellement dû à la différence entre la conception du développement chez les populations concernées par le développement et celle des développeurs souvent déterminés par l'action du capital transnational et des intérêts camouflés de ces derniers »).

But generally, intellectual activity displayed during the 1950's and 1960's under the United Nations to study the problem of underdevelopment was unprecedented. It is at that time that were born the most diverse theories about development. These are vicious circle theories, sociological and psychosocial theories; dualistic theories (Boeke and Higgins, Meier and Eckhaus) and finally the theory growth steps (Rostow), not to mention other more partial views (Mynt, Viner, Baldwin), etc. All these theories, very different in terms of scientific value, but with scattered undeniable value, had one common point. That of analyzing underdevelopment by taking the developed capitalist societies as a point of reference, if not as a model. The emergence of new conceptual perspectives and orientation shift appeared in the late 1960s and early 1970s.

The Soviet researcher Iraida Aleshina present an exhaustive and rigorous analysis of new ideas which, from that time began to prevail over the old conceptions of development. Thus, through the efforts of agencies of the United Nations, a new body of theory emerged . . . and actually led to very controversial ideas . . . This is an amazing phenomenon, that the change such on an issue as fundamental as the concept of development be operated for a short time. Moreover, new perspectives (new approaches to development) have varied so radically from the previously dominant criterion which considered development as synonymous with growth, and most importantly, researchers did not seek to replace the old simplistic and unilateral theory "Growth = Development" by another equally homogeneous thesis. On the contrary, there has been a real emergence of different interpretations, a sort of ferment of new ideas, now reconciled, sometimes contradictory, and some ephemeral and seldom followed; other more persistent and more widely adopted, but all carry a much richer content, more complex and deeper than the theory that prevailed at the earlier time. It is thus emerged and began to confront various concepts such as integrated development and human-centered development, harmonized development (G.C.Sebregondi), harmonized integral development (L.J.Lebret), endogenous development, global development, unified development, self-sufficiency (self-reliance), development strategy based on basic needs (basic) and probably on another level, sustainable development, combining environment and development, global development (New International Economic Order) and globalization. The question that arises is: to know where this change so noticeable by its quick widespread as well as by its innovative and varied conceptual depth comes from. One thing is certain: this change is not accidental and the quick widespread as well as the diversity of its conceptual manifestations have not been either. However, it can be stated that the factors that have determined it are at least as important as the change itself. It is important to note that developing countries have been the subject of a development process which ejected them more and more from the international capital flows and trade. These two most important supports of neo-colonialism began to crumble with no opportunity to find other perspectives. In addition, according to Oscar Pino Santos, neo-colonialism has not created an external economic frame appropriate to development. This was evident during the 60s when, on the one hand, the theory based on the equation "Growth = Development" has led to an impasse and, on the other hand, it has even been noticed a rejection phenomenon against the economic mechanisms and arguments which were based on this system.

The So-called assistance or development aid proved to be a more effective mechanism to maintain links of interest in favor of former colonizers; but it was soon noticed that the relationship did not meet the needs of recipient countries, qualitatively or quantitatively. By this mechanism of development aid is born a new form of economic dependence characterized by excessive debt in developing countries, which led Alidou Sawadogo to state *(«(. . .) our countries are deeply endebted, some will not be able to reimburse their debts even by the time of resurrection! And all this to pay for a Western-style development» (. . .) nos pays sont endettés, certains ne rembourseront même pas leurs dettes d'ici la résurrection! Et cela pour se payer un développement à l'occidentale »).* The emphasis on industrialization at the expense of agriculture and rural development, has in several cases led to rural exodus, unplanned urbanization and a decrease in food production, the effects of which are in many Third world and especially African countries currently experienced. Thus, many discussions have led to new ideas such as integrated rural development and basic needs. Other ideas have also been devoted in recent years, to the development of a new order that would gradually eliminate poverty and its causes, a goal that is very different from that which is to provide direct assistance to those starving people. But all these thoughts, ideas and concepts are not left without comment. For example, Mohamed Cisse said: « (. . .) *food aid makes you lazy one tends to always rely on assistance. Food aid was used to create markets for western wheat. Before, we were not used to eating it. It's the same with milk powder».* « (. . .) *l'aide alimentaire rend paresseux. On a toujours tendance à se reposer sur l'aide. L'aide alimentaire a été utilisée pour créer des marchés pour le blé occidental. Avant, on n'était pas habitué à le consommer. C'est la même chose avec le lait en poudre »).* And a farmer said: « (. . .) *Food aid causes people to sleep, while in donor countries, people work like machines; they store, they do not know what to do with surpluses . . . Ultimately, aid increases dependency»*[23] *(«(. . .) L'aide alimentaire pousse les gens à dormir, alors que dans les pays donateurs, les gens travaillent comme des machines. Ils stockent, ils ne savent que faire des excédents . . . En fin de compte, l'aide augmente la dépendance »).*

If such support is fully justified in cases of acute crisis, it is them urgent to make recourse to a more sustainable action, in the form of technical, financial and educational support, to a control techniques (concept of appropriate technology) and to structures best suited to the real needs of countries, to generate a real development process concerned with the balance between growth and resource levels. In this historical development of different concepts, which characterize the orientation of development ideas, another concept emerged as requirements expressing and characterizing at the same time the claim of developing countries. It is the establishing of a new world economic order. This concept of new world economic order is in fact a program for restructuring the international economic relations. The new international economic order is probably the issue that has been the most debated within the international community. This question is at the forefront of development. It is confirmed that international relations, in their current manifestations, constitute an obstacle to the development process in the South and perpetuate the dependence of these countries and the maintenance of neo-colonialism. The consideration of this claim in the South has largely contributed to create a universal awareness of this contemporary tragedy represented by the delay and poverty an which most of humanity, contrasting with the development of productive forces, the scientific, technical, economic level and living standards achieved by a minority in favor which the

---

[23] Un paysan Mossi du Yatenga cité par P. PRADERVAND, op.cit., p.336.

advantages of civilization are concentrated[24]. The new direction of development that is proposed here, that of conscious development, partly addresses this concern, because the imbalance at the level of resource exploitation, the cult of economic growth, human survival, poverty and environmental degradation are all factors that require a change in development direction. Given the weight of setbacks on the ground in the past, the theories in question have not stood the test of a critical epistemological tight, solely motivated by a desire to define the ideal conditions for successful development of specific characteristics.

---

[24] O.P.SANTOS, op.cit., p. 235.

Chapter III

THE CONSCIOUS DEVELOPMENT

Development without conscience is ruin communities.

3.1. INTRODUCTION

We have just examined the various concepts that have guided to date researcher's thinking on the development. The concepts and theories that have been just examined a little have distorted a little reality in their application, but they allow to identify the underlying trends in complex historical situations. They provide a conceptual framework that helps us to analyze specific situations as development programming must be based on facts as experienced by communities. The development process requires concrete action, but this action is always preceded by theoretical thinking, as stated by A. Einstein: « *Imagination is more important than knowledge*[25] ». Development requires imagination in the search of ways and means. David John Farmer said: « *It speaks about institutionalizing imagination* »[26]. This is to institutionalize or better to use imagination in development practice. Theoretical reflection serves to circumscribe the framework within which the development action to undertake is planned. It can guide science, it always precedes the action to undertake, but the « *the thinking on development does not need, to go ahead, of a preliminary accurate action, and therefore of a strictly*

---

[25]   A. COOK, American Accent Training, Barron's Educational Series, NY, 1989, p.20.

[26]   D. J. FARMER, To Kill the King. Post-traditional Governance and Bureaucracy, Ed. M.E.Sharpe, New York, 2005, p.xi.

defined concept of development; directions are sufficient»[27] *(« réflexion sur le développement n'a pas besoin, pour se poursuivre, d'une mesure préalable exacte, et donc d'un concept strictement défini du développement; des directions suffisent »).* It is within this framework that we propose two new concepts, which give in a certain way, the new directions of thinking, designing and directing the development process: conscious development and development monad model. Conscious development and development monad model fall within the same school of thought than the above concepts with the same concern to better understand and guide the actions of development within the constraints and demands of the moment.

More facts and realities could, in given time and space, inspire further guidance or development concepts. This evidences the relativity of the development process, as Joan Robinson said:

"The fate of the economic theory has been that of losing breath in an already lost race against history without being able to complete the analysis of an economic development step before another succeeds". The ideal order of knowledge production would like that the analysis of factual data comes before the theory, but the reality of facts is the appropriate level of analysis. Development as an interdisciplinary social science, is mainly intended to, the identification of political, institutional, socio-economic, cultural, environmental processes . . . capable of causing in human corporations or communities the structural changes needed to bring to the majority of the population an overall welfare. As an empirical science, development seeks to understand, predict and control observable events. To achieve this goal, it sets models and theories that it controls through assumptions. Models and theories will not help to develop rigid scientific laws and universal truths as the physical sciences.

---

[27]   E. ASSIDON, Les théories économiques du développement, Ed.La Découverte, Paris, 1992, p.102.

Its laws are trends wide variation according to cultures, space (country, region, area), time or given period." (« *Le sort de la théorie économique a été de s'essouffler dans une course perdue d'avance contre l'histoire sans être capable d'achever l'analyse d'une phase du développement économique avant qu'une autre ne lui ait succédé* ». *L'ordre idéal de la production du savoir voudrait que l'analyse des données factuelles précède la théorie, mais la réalité concrète des faits constitue le niveau d'analyse pertinent. Le développement, comme science sociale interdisciplinaire, se veut comme tâche principale, l'identification des processus politiques, institutionnels, socio-économiques, culturels, environnementaux . . . aptes à provoquer sur des sociétés ou communautés humaines les transformations structurelles nécessaires pour apporter à la plus grande partie de la population son bien-être global. En tant que science empirique, le développement cherche à comprendre, à prévoir et à contrôler les événements observables. Pour atteindre cet objectif, il pose des modèles et des théories qu'il vérifie par des hypothèses. Les modèles et théories ne permettront pas d'arriver à des lois scientifiques rigides et des vérités universelles comme en sciences physiques. Ses lois sont des tendances susceptibles d'une grande variation selon les cultures, l'espace (pays, région, zone), le temps ou l'époque donnée.* »)

It is therefore necessary to ask and answer the question of whether there should be one or more theories. The answer to this question suggests an adaptation of the theory to specific circumstances and time. The concept of conscious development we offer meets this requirement. Conscious development and development monad model will apply taking into account the specificities of the communities studied.

3.2. <u>CONSCIOUS DEVELOPMENT</u>

Conscious development can be defined as a process of conscious imagination but also a permanent state of mind, which, through education, aims at promoting the overall welfare of communities.

3.2.1. <u>DETERMINING FACTOR</u>

In his reflection on the search for a development paradigm, Hirschman writes, « *At the end it will be possible to have a kind of social science that would be very different from what most of us have practiced; a moral-social science . . . where moral considerations will no longer of us have practiced, or be expressed unconsciously, but may be exposed openly and innocently. This is in fact the social science that I dream for our grandchildren*» (« *Au bout du chemin il sera alors possible d'apercevoir une sorte de science sociale qui serait très différente de celle que la plupart d'entre nous ont pratiquée; une science moralo-sociale . . . où les considérations morales n'auront plus besoin d'être introduites en fraude, ni d'être exprimées inconsciemment, mais pourront être exposées ouvertement et innocemment. Voici en tout cas la science sociale dont je rêve pour nos petits-enfants* »). Consciousness is defined as *moral sensibility established in us by the habits we have taken as a result our education. (comme une sensibilité morale établie en nous par les habitudes que nous avons prises suite à notre éducation*). Maharishi thinks that the determining factor in quality of life in a society, is the level of coherence or integration of the collective consciousness. According to him, the result of a coherent collective consciousness is the integration of individual desires with the needs of the society. The ability to spontaneously meet one's own interests, while contributing to achieving the interest of society, depends on the level of identification of individual consciousness.

There is therefore a close relationship between the quality of social life and the ability of individuals to create an effect of integration in the collective consciousness[28]. We believed that the current development of facts and realities of development leads us to consider a new direction of development where the moral and ethical or moral-social according to Hirschman's expression should help to restore the balance between the aspect of economic growth in development and the balance level of resources and environment. It is based on the interrelationship between these three elements: communities (population), resources (environment), development (development resources) that we will define the new direction of development, namely conscious development and development monad model.

3.2.2. <u>FOUNDATIONS</u>

The historical development of ideas on development proves us that development is a historical process. For any given historical period, the facts required a new orientation of ideas on development. And this new development approach stems from the perception of new needs expressed by the community. Thus were born the various concepts of development that we analyzed above. It is believed that the current reality of facts requires a new focus on development not in terms of neocolonialism or dependency from south to north, or from poverty, etc., but from questions on which depends humans king survival where are involved Northern countries as well as southern ones, in short, human communities. As has been highlighted by M.Bellman Geoffrey

---

[28] M. MAHESH YOGI, Life Supported by Natural Law, Washington DC, Age of Enlightenment Press, 1986, p.74.

that, « *Ideas must find their time* »[29]. Powerful nations rise and fall, brave men and women give their lives to a noble cause, but great ideas can last forever. So we need to change our way of thinking and approaching development problems. On this, A.Einstein states, « *one cannot solve a problem with the same kind of thinking that gave rise to the problem* »[30]. And as usual, « problems are often poorly solved because initially, they are misunderstood ». As has often been confirmed, human economic activity is changing at a very high speed the very conditions that sustain life on earth and the resulting transformations may yield catastrophic consequences on communities[31].

For example, In spite of hope and all expectations, the concept of sustainable development has failed. The reality is more twenty years after the world summit of Rio (1992), the state of the planet has worsened and continues to worsen. Some of the most significant international agreements addressing the challenges facing our planet were developed 20 years ago when the world's leaders met in Rio de Janeiro. The current system of human development, based on increased consumption and reliance on fossil fuels, combined with a growing human population and poor overall management and governance of natural resources, is unsustainable[32]. Conscious development would address this concern that alters the conditions of economic and community development. For Stephen C.Smith, « *Poverty can be eliminated in a surprisingly short time, if we focus on the problem . . . ending poverty is possible . . . create a moral imperative for action* »[33]. The concept of conscious

---

[29]   G. M. BELHMAN, Getting Things Done When You are not in Charge, Berret-Koehler publishers, San-Francisco, 1992, p. 84.

[30]   A. EINSTEIN, cité par A.COOK, op.cit., p.20.

[31]   C. VILLENEUVE, op.cit., p.19.

[32]   WWF, Living Planet Report 2012,op.cit., p.10.

[33]   S. C. SMITH, Ending Global Poverty, Ed.Palgrave, New York, 2005, p.6.

development is comprehensive in terms of the interrelationships of facts and evidence (growth, development, resources, communities, environment) that characterize it. In this new direction of development that we propose, it is to reconcile the moral and ethical, socio-economic and environmental imperatives. We believe that at this time of history, the factor "consciousness" must be considered in the development process in the same way as other development factors such as income, consumption, poverty, population, savings and investment, market, production, globalization, science and technology, etc.

It is important to remind the scientific opinion expressed by the Vezelay group that the planet is sick, and that for the first time in history, human activity may alter irreversibly the fundamental balance necessary for life[34]. It is also important to know that *"our wealth, health and well-being are dependent on ecosystem services. Many areas of high biodiversity also provide important ecosystem services such as carbon storage, fuel wood, freshwater flow and fish stocks. Human activities are affecting the continued provision of these services. Deforestation and forest degradation currently account for up to 20% of global anthropogenic co^2 emissions, including losses from forest soils. Only a third of the world's rivers that are longer than 1,000 km are free flowing and without dams on their main channel. A nearly five-fold increase in global marine fish catch, from 19 million tonnes in 1950 to 87 million tonnes in 2005, has left many fisheries overexploited. The frequency and complexity of land use competition will rise as human demands grow.*

Throughout the developing world, there is an unprecedented rush by outside investors to secure access to land for future food and fuel production. The loss of biodiversity and its related ecosystem services particularly impacts

---

[34]   Le Groupe de Vézelay cité par J. KI-ZERBO, op.cit., p.7.

the poor, who rely most directly on these services to survive"[35]. According to Ervin Laszlo and Peter Seidel, « *ethics are the minimum standards that make a collective life possible . . . The world is in need of an ethical base on which to stand* »[36].

The petition signed by 1,670 scientists in 1993, including 102 Nobel Prize, declared, among other things, « *a new ethic is required* ». Thus, increased awareness, as a development factor, is imperative and urgent, this requires the involvement of all the communities. And as Frances Beale says, « *To wage a revolution, we need competent teachers, doctors, nurses, electronics experts, chemists, biologists, physicists, political scientists, and so on and so forth* » [37] We believe that economic growth, an important development factor, but not the only one, must be shaped by the increasing awareness in the community development process. If different realities of historical facts as the concern for environmental conservation, neo-colonialism, the North-South dialogue, international aid, economic dependence, growth, etc., inspired different concepts and theories of development such as sustainable development, endogenous development, self-reliant development, the dependency theory, Rostow's growth stages theory, etc., it is clear that the current concerns of communities favor a new design or development orientation. Community concerns as expressed and supported such, as the future of the planet and human survival, improvement of living conditions of communities, the level of resources and environment, have led to conscious development and monad model of development. The concept of conscious development, far from being an intellectual utopia, would reconcile the physical (growth), social and cultural development aspects

---

[35]   WWF, Living Planet Report 2012, in www.wwf.org, p.13.

[36]   E. LASLO and P. SEIDEL, Global Survival, Selectbooks, New York, 2006, p.117.

[37]   F. BEALE cité par D. ALTMAN, op.cit., p.50.

in the context and purpose of development characterized not only by the economic growth and the acquisition of material goods, but also by moral, spiritual, ethical and social aspects, as claimed by some authors such as Donella and Aurelio Pecci, « *never failed to conclude that the answers to the world's problems begin with a new humanism* »[38] (*Ne jamais faillir de conclure que les réponses aux problèmes mondiaux commencent par un nouvel humanisme*).

A group of Nobel Prize laureates scientists gathered in Rome in November 2003 stated that: « *ethics in the relations between nations and in government policies is of paramount importance. Nations must treat other nations as they wish to be treated* »[39]. Conscious development is essentially characterized by its comprehensiveness, since it includes all the features of other development concepts discussed above emphasizing that any development, to be endogenous, sustainable, comminatory, integrated, etc . . . Must above all be aware, because it is awareness, and awareness alone, which should allow the realization of the objectives of the different communities. Development without awareness is characterized by reckless and irresponsible acts that can be illustrated according to African wisdom by the following behavior: *One upon a time, there was in a village, a man who was breeding snakes in his house. One day, villagers people heard about the death of this man. One of the residents wanted to know the cause of his death. One of the village elders will said, when one breed snakes in his house (which is an irresponsible and thoughtless act), should you ask the cause of his death? It has to be understood that snakes killed him.* Awareness involves thoughtful acts, but also other moral values such as responsibility, truth and justice, will, determination, courage, selflessness, sacrifice, patriotism and nationalism, etc.

---

[38] J. RANDERS and D. MEADOWS, Limits to Growth, Chelsea Green Publishing, USA, 2004, p.282.

[39] E. LASLO, op.cit., p.117.

3.2.3. <u>ISSUES</u>

The importance of some issues raised in the introduction is such that it is not possible to solve these problems just at a local level (area) or even at regional or national level. The seriousness of such issues and the complex relationship they have with the physical, social and human development require a new type of development that, we are advocating here, namely conscious development. So we dare say that if the different approaches to development previously used have almost failed, it is because the effort was mainly focused on the growth or economic development aspect than on the consciousness development in development. Otherwise it would be difficult to explain the fact that man is endangering his own survival by his activities, especially by his economic activities. On this, let us remind for example, that the U.S. President George W. Bush Jr. will refuse to sign the Kyoto Protocol only because the American comfort is not negotiable. He favors American citizens interests at the expense of the planet survival.

Neil Postman says, « *Technology makes life easier, cleaner, and longer, but it creates a culture without a moral foundation and undermines the very things that make life worth living* »[40]. The concept of development, as currently envisaged at different levels of the community action and that is directed exclusively in the direction of economic growth, now seems to be seriously questioned mainly in the light of experiences drawn from decades of development and of its current impact on the overall development of communities. There is today a need for some realism as outlined by Larry Bossidy, « *realism is the heart of execution, but many organizations are full of people who are trying to avoid or shade*

---

[40]   M. J. MANDEL, Rational Exuberance. Silencing the Enemies of Growth and Why the Future is Better than You Think, Ed. HarperBusiness, New York, 2004, p.79.

reality . . . they want to hide mistakes »[41]. The purely economic conception of development is in crisis today because the trend of excessive accumulation of goods and services, which characterizes our economic system does not achieve the overall welfare of the communities, despite the many material benefits that science and technology continue to provide us with. And it is becoming increasingly clear that the serious current problems of humanity are not scientific or technological, but moral, because if they were scientific or technological, we could have already solved them as stated by Loron Wade that: « *So why do we still have hunger, violence, tyranny Because the worst problems of the age are not scientific but moral problems. If they were scientific or technological problems, we would have solved them long ago. We are really good at that* »[42]. The previous decades experience on development proves instead that if the entire available amount of resources and potential within the community is not governed by rules or moral values, on the one hand, and an orientation towards the community welfare, on the other hand, this amount of resources is but a source of oppression against the communities. The wealth that could have contributed to the welfare of communities is rather a source of domination and oppression. This is the case of oil, as Michel Collon states: « *If you want to rule the world, you need to control oil. All oil. Anywhere* »[43]. But according to the new vision of president Barrack Obama, It's imperative "*to move beyond mindset of perpetual war*".

---

[41] L. BOSSILY and R. CHARAN, Execution. The Discipline of Getting Things Done, Crown Business, 2002, p.67.

[42] L. WADE, The Ten Commandements, Ed.Gerald Wheeler, USA, 2006, p.128.

[43] M.COLLON cité par D.ICKE, Tales From the Time Sloop. The Most Comprehensive Exposé of the Global Conspiracy Ever Written and all you Need to Know to be Truly Free ; Ed.Bridge of love publications, USA, 2003, p.68.

Wealth, for example, finances wars that destroy lives and are the source of innumerable miseries, generates unrest, source of insecurity, supports and encourages rebellions in Africa, destabilizes democratically elected regimes, etc . . . Yet, *«the possession of goods does not necessarily improve the owner unless it contributes to his maturation and enrichment, in other words, to the fulfillment of his human vocation»*[44] (*« avoir des biens ne perfectionne pas en soi le sujet humain si cela ne contribue pas à la maturation et à l'enrichissement de son être, c'est-à-dire à la réalisation de la vocation humaine en tant que telle »*). According to Martin Luther King Jr. : Injustice anywhere is injustice everywhere". We are thus faced with two development levels or systems, namely the over-development, characterized by overproduction and overconsumption, and underdevelopment, characterized by under-consumption and under-production, with the result that wealth, but not necessarily happiness or welfare, is the consequence of the first (overdevelopment) and poverty is the direct consequence of the other (underdevelopment). Overdevelopment, which characterizes the societies in the North, is reflected in the obsession of acquiring excessive material goods and services by some groups in the society (politicians and especially company owners) some people become thus slaves of their goods and immediate enjoyment, regardless of the fact that the multiplication of these goods and the continual replacement of those already owned by other still more sophisticated goods and at an irrational pace, contributes to the accelerated depletion of the Earth resources. Overconsumption or the mass consumer society advocated by Rostow is characterized by an ever-increasing production and an always overestimated consumption at the expense of the level and quality of resources used, it is also characterized by the production of too much waste which is the basis of

---

[44]   Pape JEAN PAUL II, op.cit.p.57.

other forms of pollution. A still more characteristic of this addition to overconsumption, is «(. . .) *this crude materialism which is at the same time a radical dissatisfaction for the more you have, the more you want, while the true aspirations of the development of the majority of people remain unsatisfied and even stifled».* (. . .) *cette forme de matérialisme grossier qui est en même temps une insatisfaction radicale, car plus on possède, plus on désire, tandis que les aspirations profondes du développement de la majorité des populations restent insatisfaites et même étouffées »).* This is contrary to the "Ne Kongo" wisdom which emphasizes the sense of sharing, in this proverb « *dia lungila kansi kayukuta ko* ».

According to this adage, eating is sharing and not satisfying one's greed. Food (wealth) must first be shared among all the members before satisfying one's personal needs alone. So there is a need to introduce a new type of development more conscious and concerned about the use of our resources, because the current development model, which characterizes our communities, is one in which the sole purpose is to promote the economic growth and development. Its purpose is not come to a kind of a balance, but rather to achieve economic performance, of which the consequences are overproduction, overconsumption, excessive indebtedness, etc . . . Globally, the current development model, characterized by the growth of economic performance and liberalism, has very little concern about the level of resources and their depletion. When one observes the quantities of goods exhibited in supermarkets and most of which is doomed to destruction at their expiry date, one has to wonder about the rate of our resources depletion. Pope Jean Paul II stresses that, *«The evil does not consist in "having goods" as such but in the fact of getting goods in a way that does not meet the quality nor the order of value property, value quality and order which arise from the subordination of goods and making them available to the "welfare" of man and his true vocation. The exclusive pursuit of "acquiring goods" is therefore an obstacle to man's growth and is opposite to his true value. For nations as well as for individuals, avarice is the most obvious form of moral underdevelopment.* (« *Le mal ne consiste pas dans l' « avoir » en tant que tel mais dans le fait de posséder d'une façon qui ne respecte pas la qualité ni l'ordre des valeurs des biens que l'on a, qualité et ordre des valeurs qui découlent de la subordination des biens et de leur mise à la disposition de l' « être » de l'homme et de sa vraie vocation. La recherche exclusive de l' « avoir » fait dès lors obstacle à la croissance de l'être et s'oppose à sa véritable grandeur. Pour les nations comme pour les personnes, l'avarice est la forme la plus évidente du sous-développement moral* »). Thus, it is clear that if development has a necessary economic dimension, since it must make available, for the largest possible number of inhabitants of the world, goods and services essential to man, it does not unfortunately be limited to an economic dimension. Conscious development would set in its approach, the balance between the economic and ethico social development characteristic.

Conscious development, which seeks this balance, focuses on economic development considerations which should promote the moral feature through education. This is as stated by Pope Jean Paul II, to become aware of the fact that no one can use with impunity the different categories of beings (animals, plants, . . .) as he wants and sometimes in a selfish way, that is to say, according to his own economic needs and regardless of the nature of each being and his interaction with the environment (ecosystem) to become aware of the limited natural resources of which some are not renewable; to realize that using them as if they were unlimited, not only jeopardizes their availability not only for the present generation but also for future generations according to the concept of sustainable development; finally, to consider the consequences of a certain type of development on the quality of life. These are the consequences of excessive industrialization on environmental pollution, the consequences of overconsumption on health, of overproduction and its impact on the accelerated degradation and depletion of resources, etc . . . This need to acquire as much property as possible, sometimes without moderation, is the basis of the following adverse consequences that characterize our world today: the increase in poverty as the rich become richer and richer the poor poorer, and the lack of consideration the minority interests; exaggerated exploitation of resources and their degradation; the various conflicts of interest arising from the acquisition of wealth; contempt for universal values and the economic and military domination.

3.2.4. OBJECTIVES

In the following lines, we will present the new development objectives and conscious development objectives.

1. NEW DEVELOPMENT GOALS

Conscious development proposes a new direction to development goals, objectives directed toward the realization of the moral and spiritual welfare as well as to the material welfare as is currently observed and undergone through the planet. We believe that mankind has accumulated enough material wealth and that the real problem today is the fair distribution of all this wealth in the world. The more unfair a society is, the more urgent to enhance equity, if we really want to reduce poverty. A balance must therefore be set between the various developments objectives.

Communities face today, in the field of economic activities that contribute to their development, an unprecedented situation in which the stakes are very high for their development. It is more necessary than ever to increase the economic activity in a fairer and more rational way in order to meet the basic needs of the growing communities and ensure their overall welfare. A major concern, which is currently reflected in the demands from developing countries is the setting of a new economic and political world. This claim comprises two interrelated aspects, one of which is essentially political and the other is rather economical. But beyond these two aspects, political and economic, it is the questioning of the development process which is concerned. Indeed, the level of poverty is growing more and more, while the level of resources displays permanent deterioration, along with a continued degradation of the environment. In the same order, it is noticed that those who are economically and hence politically powerful, both at the national and regional or trans-regional levels, persist in their interest to create and disseminate ideological, political and economic conditions likely to perpetuate that power. Globalization has just reinforced their power. Conversely, those who hold the economic and political power in developing are reluctant and refuse to accept a new direction of development of which the analysis or action would seek to provide the elucidation of the mechanisms by which states or communities that they represent persist in the situation of underdevelopment, poverty, countries dominated by imperialism[45], etc . . . In fact, both aspects, political and economic, are manifested in the form of protest action to defend the interests of developing countries against developed countries, as part of a denunciation of injustice of the current international economic system. These are claims aimed at, inter alia, the international monetary system, international trade, and technology transfer and development cooperation. Conscious development does not only consider these two aspects of the new world economic order, which characterize the

---

[45]   O. P. SANTOS, op.cit., p.222.

claims of the South against the North. It encompasses all the aspects of development that characterize both the North and South. These are mainly problems of development, population and environment, which are global issues, they concern the North and South, and upon which depend the very survival of humankind in general. Here, reference can be made to the balance between growth (development) and the level of economic resources. Conscious development applies because of its requirements towards all the communities, those of the North as well as those of the South.

The same issue concerns level of our behavior opposite the exploitation of our resources and of some economic practices harmful to these resources. In this regard, the same problem arises in both North and South, actively for some and passively for others. This requires, Ervin Laszlo writes, « *a public morality, the ethic shared in our community, ethnic group, state, or nation . . . a universal morality, a planetary ethic.* In the state-of-the matter, we specified that man economic activity both in the world and locally become an obstacle to development. The material over enrichment constitutes an obstacle to spiritual and moral development of people and communities.

2. CONSCIOUS DEVELOPMENT OBJECTIVES

The development objective in a society is to provide its members with a better quality of life. In this perspective, this means to meet the needs of individuals and communities while ensuring the sustainability of society and to give the structures and the corresponding means to achieve this objective[46]. To achieve the objective of development set out above, development should be primarily a conscious act, because

---

[46]   C. VILLENEUVE, op.cit., p.45.

development without conscience is but the ruin of communities. It is through conscious acts in everyday life characterized by political will that we can help achieve the objective of all development. One goal of conscious development is to come to break the inability in which the communities of North and South are deeply rooted, inability that prevents them from understanding the serious problems that threaten our existence on the one hand, and our harmonious development, on the other hand. Education seems to be, therefore, the most appropriate way to achieve this goal. It is also the most likely to achieve the objective of development, which is the people's welfare, and this, by modeling the behavior of individuals and communities through the acquisition of moral values essential to the progress of the individual himself, his community and society. The aim of conscious development is no different from the overall objective of the development process, that of improving people and communities living conditions, because our great wealth would be useless if the different communities were to remain marginalized.

From the perspective of conscious development, real development is that which enables individuals to make choices, that is to say development choices in the direction of the positive act, which contributes to the promotion and development, or negative act, which contributes to the regression of the individual or community. Of course, no one can guarantee human happiness and it is up to each person to decide on his life, but the development process should at least create an environment that would give individuals and communities a chance to realize their potential and lead to a creative and productive life in accordance with their needs and interests[47]. According to C.S Lewis, "*there are far better things ahead than any we leave behind*". Development is no longer an

---

[47]   PNUD, op.cit., p.6.

act of disordered accumulation of wealth, it must mainly be concerned with what is good for man in his community. It is consciousness, and consciousness alone, which will determine all other positive aspects of development, that is, those that contribute to real progress of individuals and communities. Thus, the conscious development process, planned and designed in this way, implies a decorum, that is to say a set of rules to be observed in a good community, thanks to the educational activity which constitutes its foundation. It is therefore a kind of development more concerned and more aware of our daily actions and in all areas of economic, cultural, social, moral, political activities, where human intervention is necessary. This is act a valued daily act which helps us to promote our own development (welfare), because « *It does not develop, it develops* »[48]. The action of development which helps to promote our development sometimes begins with a simple act but which is important in the development process, for example, the will or the worry to empty the trash cans, not in the street but in a public dumping, to willingly refuse and consciously refuse to eat foods exhibited along the highway, to avoid consuming drugs sold on the street, to favor public interest instead of personal interest, to refrain from setting fire to forests and bush, etc. Since "any human act has its positive and negative side", in terms of conscious development, "good act is one that has the most positive effect", that is to say, one that contributes to the promoting the welfare of the individual and the community.

Whereas, "bad act is the one which produces the most negative and least positive effect" to promote the welfare of the individual and of the community, but also *«which comprises a higher proportion of inevitable negative effects»*[49] (« *qui admet une part de négatif plus*

---

[48] R. M. MBAYA, op.cit., p.10.

[49] J. M. VAN PARYS, Petite introduction à l'éthique, Ed. Loyola, Kinshasa, p.14.

importante que l'inévitable »). It is therefore up to the individual conscience and the community to appreciate what is positive what is negative involved in the development process on a daily basis. Since these acts stem and take their origin from the individuals minds, it is there that they are to be fought, thanks to the educational development as recommended by conscious development. For this reason, given this reality, we advocate the monad model of development that takes into account the specificities of each community from the monad as a basic community unit, because development is a "social" logic. It is up to each community, according to its cultural specificity, to assess and adopt what is good and positive for its promotion and development, and reject what is bad and negative, that leads to its decline. Given this "socio" logic specificity of development, we understand why conscious development, to be realized, relies on the development monad model. Conscious development emphasizes development that is rooted at the base, because the current development models as they are designed, implemented and realized at the community level are those whose orientation is determined from above by politicians according to their economic, financial, military and political interests. These models are appreciated from above to the extent that they realize or guarantee the major macroeconomic balances which, incidentally are made and broken up according to the interests of funds donor, powerful countries, important corporations, etc . . . But, as stated by Donald Kennedy, « *In a world solely governed by the principle of "dog eats dog"* »[50] [51] the change of mentality, which should result in a new conception of objectives and

---

[50] D. KENNEDY, State of the Planet 2006-2007, Islandpress, Washington DC, 2006, p.121.

[51] This to remind the congolese song from the congolese artist singer Luambo Makiadi FRANCO « BOMA NGAI NA BOMA YO TOBOMANA, it means "kill me, I kill you and we kill each other ».

development guidelines, has to be initiated by communities through educational activity and result in our daily actions. Even in wartime, the best defense of a country consists of its population. This is the same for development. It is necessary that the whole population join the objectives set for development, but for this change of mentality and the accession of the population, it is important to promote education of the population, because only people educational can lead to a change and a mobilization of energies needed in the development process.

Conscious development emphasizes the need to invest in the individual (community), that is to say, his education, his health and material living conditions so that he be finally able to contribute to production (economic growth). Education is thus crucial in the process of conscious development, because it alone can enable the individual or the community to understand the merits of his actions and his involvement in the development process and especially to make their choices. In the current situation, as highlighted by the UNDP, *«the best asset of a nation lies in education, in addition, investment in education in general (education and technology) can shorten the steps of progress. Investment in education is, whatever the country, one of the most appropriate strengths. An educated and literate population is more productive and contributes more to economic growth»*[52] (« *le meilleur atout d'une nation réside dans le niveau d'éducation, par ailleurs, les investissements en éducation en général (enseignement et en technologie) permettent de raccourcir les étapes du progrès. L'investissement dans l'éducation est, quel que soit le pays, l'un des plus judicieux atouts qui soit. Une population instruite et éduquée est plus productive et contribue davantage à la croissance économique* ») and to the development process. This is consistent with the monad basic model of development, which is based on a development based on socio-cultural

---

[52]   PNUD, op.cit.p.6.

communities specificities as delimited by their geo-ethnic, tribal areas, because what is accepted in a community may be rejected by another. However, to according the concept of conscious development, every man must be able, through education, to distinguish in any development activity to be undertaken, good and bad, positive and negative acts, because *«the sense of right and evil is characteristic of every man as such in possession of his faculties»* (*« le sens du bien et du mal est propre à tout homme en tant que tel en possession de ses facultés »*). For example, The same sex marriage condemned in the bible by God is now accepted in many countries of Europe and USA. This discernment of development activities to be undertaken, is what that is referred to in this dissertation: the conscious positive activities and negative conscious activities. The development process (embodied by the development activities to be undertaken) is one whose purpose is reflected in the mutual promotion and enhancement of communities while current development models in our country and even globally have more privileged individuals to the detriment of communities.

The consequence of these development models dominated and dictated primarily by economic liberalism is that a tiny minority has monopolized the country and world wealth at the expense of the poverty of the majority. This inequality requires from the people and communities a lifetime training to become informed, educated, responsible and committed citizens, able to think, act and find creative solutions to solve problems of development, population and environment. This requires that individuals and citizens are endowed with a culture which is not only scientific but also moral and social, and they are able and willing to engage in individual or collective actions for development. Conscious development would restore and sustain the positive relationship between the individual, the community, nature, resources and environment. It would be necessary that any definition of the development action, whose objective is above all man and his future, take into account our positive relationship with the biophysical environment to which we belong and on which our existence depends.

3.2.5. <u>EDUCATION AS A BASIS FOR DEVELOPMENT</u>

The objectives of conscious development require educational activities (awareness, animation, popularization, etc.) at the community level through formal education as well as through informal education, becauseaccording to Van Parys *«if any same person can naturally also have a sense of what is right and wrong, the judgments of different people on the same situations are not always the same as the practical application of right and wrong depends on circumstances, places and times»* (*« si tout homme sain d'esprit a naturellement le sens du bien et du mal, les jugements des différentes personnes sur les mêmes situations ne sont pas toujours les mêmes étant donné que l'application pratique du bon et du mauvais est très variable selon les circonstances, les lieux et les époques »*). This confirms that development is a "social" logics because what is accepted by a community may be rejected by another. The interdependence between conscious development and the monad model of development is thus characteristic at the level of education to which they resort. It mainly refers to traditional education and environmental education. Traditional education is specific to each community, while environmental education is specific to each environment (milieu).

The monad model of development and conscious development are interdependent, in that the foundation of education, the basis of conscious development, and environment, as a geo-physical space, are specific to each ethnic, tribal, clanic or familial community. For example, the traditional and environmental education of a "libinza" child (libinza are coastal people) will be different from that "Mukongo" child (people of Savannah), due to the specific socio-cultural and environmental of the two communities. Therefore, due to the cultural clanic, tribal or ethnic, regional or local specifities the assessment of development activities has different meanings from one community to another, from one period to another, because the motives of one given community, clan, tribe or ethnic in one given area (country, region) are not always the same. In addition, customs are not always uniform everywhere. What is accepted or tolerated by some groups may be considered a crime by others. These differences in the assessment of the activities are due to specific socio-cultural differences, changes through which universal values are noticed and accepted on the one hand, and on the other hand, the historical conditions that inform or veil some aspects of these situations. For example, what is perceived as urgent and important at a given time by the Congolese can be considered, within the same period, as less urgent by the Tutsi of Rwanda shocked by the feeling of genocide vis-à-vis their Hutu neighbors. The American or European entrepreneur who operates in a healthy economic environment does not have the same worries than the Congolese or African businessman African who works in an economic (macroeconomic) environment with inflation and instability. The Mukongo peasant from Bas-Congo, confronted to the problem of land degradation due to the bushfire, will be eager to implement agroforestry as an alternative to agriculture than the Mungala peasant of the rainforest. The interests of economic and financial countries of the North are not those of the South: the concerns of these powers are oriented towards the satisfaction of their interests and do not meet those of the poor population of the South. Given this divergence of interests, concerns and aspirations of the communities, only education can be used as a catalyst between these communities through the promotion of moral values. Unfortunately education, as an acquisition and promotion formation of moral values, is currently reduced to the level of schooling. Conscious development, of which the basis is education, is based on different educational strategies to promote development.

What is currently lacking at the level of development objectives, is the absence of moral and ethical gravity in the development process in general and in the daily behavior of communities in particular. Conscious development, which is based on community education through its various educational strategies, could bring this necessary and essential balance between the various objectives pursued by development, namely the essential material welfare, but also moral and spiritual welfare without which man can never achieve happiness, as can be read in the Bible: *«You know that the kingdom of god is not a matter of food and drink, but of right life, peace and joy in the Holy Spirit»* (*« Vous savez bien que le royaume de Dieu, n'est pas une affaire d'aliments et de boissons, mais de vie droite, de paix et de joie dans l'Esprit-Saint (Rm:14,17) »*).

3.2.6. COMPARING THE CONCEPT OF DEVELOPMENT WITH OTHER CONCEPTS AND THEORIES OF DEVELOPMENT

It has been noticed that each development concept is linked to a reality of the events that characterized the historical development of communities. Community development, for example, thus appeared during colonization. It is both a process and a method that many governments have implemented to encourage villagers to build the local initiative and energy to increase production and improve their standard of living. Endogenous development is an approach that advocates the idea of development that has an internal origin, development of which the impulse stems from within a society. Sustainable development offers a development that reflects current concerns and those of future generations. Integrated rural development, which starts from the satisfaction of the basic needs of communities, suggests a kind of development that focuses rural transformation. Integral development aims at the development of man and of every man. Eco-development is conducive to development that makes use of local solutions (local knowledge) to solve local problems. The difference between conscious development and other development concepts (community, integrated rural, full, sustainable, endogenous development . . .) is marked by its requirements first to take who account the socio-moral values essential to promoting development such as education, which is its foundation. Socio-moral values acquired through education must now guide the process action of community development.

Moreover, conscious development encompasses all other concepts because whether it is endogenous, Comminatory, sustainable, comprehensive, rural, integrated, the development process must be conscious at the outset to achieve the objective of the planned development. This is so because it is awareness that allows us to make decisions, to think, to choose our activities or our daily actions, to make comparisons or assumptions, etc . . . Conscious development can shape our "homo economicus" behavior more oriented toward the acquisition of material goods than to a behavior-based on moral and spiritual values acquired through education, to achieve the necessary and indispensable balance between the different objectives of the development, that is, the material target for material welfare, the moral target for the moral welfare, the social target for social welfare, and the spiritual target for spiritual welfare. This is not an intellectual utopia, because the purpose of education is to help people become conscious, educated and responsible of their actions. Conscious development must be practically translated into daily conscious acts through educational awareness activities and of the awareness that accompanies it. This concerns both communities in developed countries as well as those in developing countries, unlike some concepts that find their field of application only in either group. Conscious development stands opposite to concepts and theories that focus on top production at any rate, with the risk of wasting resources (economic liberalism). It is also attacks the theories and concepts that focus on the relationship between communities (producers and consumers). Finally, conscious development is not as exclusive as the theories and concepts that are concerned about the sustainability of resources. This is the case for sustainable development that proposes to leave a healthy environment to future generations.

3.2.7. <u>MORAL IMPERATIVE</u>

Conscious development offers a new vision of development action, which is not irresponsible, disorganized, individualistic and unlimited, but which is aware of all the activities carried out. Conscious development is not against economic growth and development; on the contrary, it advocates a moderate growth, which meets the level of resources and real needs of the population and a model that only seeks to satisfy the needs of a consumer society (needs positive and negative needs). Its primary purpose is the transformation of structures and mentalities for real human progress. Human progress is not limited to material progress, although the latter contributes to the satisfaction of human basic.

It is now well recognized and understood that material progress, as envisaged in the various programs and policies as development objective, has not led man to the happiness and fulfillment which he wants to achieve. Conscious development through educational activities, considers material progress as a means which should enable man to blossom, and not as the source of his misfortune due to moral loss (pride, through oppression, greed, lust for power, injustice . . .). If the drives of the humankind history required that development goals be more oriented towards the economic aspects, we find that today's development objectives must be defined in harmony with all the moral and spiritual aspects of development. The question is no more just to emphasize the economic and material aspects, but also to achieve the development goals in harmony with all the other aspects of development, especially the moral and spiritual aspects, because it is disappointing to notice that the communities wealth is used by a minority at the expense of the majority welfare. There is lack of moral responsibility on man's behalf, moral responsibility that conscious development wants to achieve through educating communities. Diamonds from Angola, for example, instead of promoting the development of the Angolan people, were rather used to finance a rebellion (UNITA) that killed people, Congolese oil has been the source of a war led by minority or a multinational group interests, to the expense of the Congolese people; the DRCongo mineral resources coltan especially are coveted by large corporations have become a source of misfortune for the Congolese people, and this is the same for Sudan oil. Speaking about Iraqi oil, Daniel Altman says: « *There may well have been economic reasons for attacking Iraq. Many critics of the administration, as they had during the first Gulf War, suspected that important unstated reasons for war were to pry open some of the world's biggest reserves of oil and natural gas, and to give business to military contractors close to the Bush administration* » [53]. Other examples can be given: the International Monetary Fund, a financial institution, which should ensure the interests of all countries, rather serves the interests of great powers; the UN has become more a

---

[53] D. ALTMAN: Neoconomy, Ed. PublicAffairs, New York, 2004, p.137.

parliament of great powers than institution for all the all the countries; the greats powers defy UN resolutions which do not meet their interests, but are struggling to enforce those imposing their will on other nations; the World Trade Organization is more an instrument of domination of the South by the North than a tool for a fair promotion of global trade.

Lies are used by superpowers to justify their acts. This has been the case to justify the Iraq invasion by the USA: « *This is why Bush, Blair, Powell and Co lied and lied and used bogus "intelligence" to desperately make a case for the war in Iraq. They didn't have a reason, so they had to invent one, as they did with Afghanistan, to follow the hidden agenda. Their first choice was "weapons of mass destruction, a term that was repeated over and over on the basis of the more times you say something the more people are likely to relieve you* »[54].

3.2.8. CONSCIOUSNESS AS A FACTOR OF GROWTH AND DEVELOPMENT

In the following paragraphs, we are going to speak of consciousness, first as a growth factor and then as a development factor.

1. CONSCIOUSNESS AS A GROWTH FACTOR

Economic growth means the continuous increase of goods and services. Throughout human history, development has been accompanied by growth. But given the results of growth on resources and community development, it has become necessary to consider an increase in awareness as a factor in economic growth. If «. . . *the mostly missing factor in developing countries, says Hirschman, is the ability to*

---

[54]   D. ICKE : op.cit., p.71.

make decision»[55] («. . . *le facteur le plus rare dans les pays en développement, affirme Hirschman, est l'aptitude à prendre des décisions* ») that is, the factor that is missing in the process of economic growth is awareness. Indeed, the problem of growth has often obeyed the criteria of economic performance (productivity), but never in harmonious conditions with the resources and environment. The economic performance criteria have led communities to practices that are economically and environmentally harmful. Growth, essential for the development of communities, can be obtained and maintained with the growth of reflective consciousness. In fact, it is the growth of awareness in production that can only contribute to economic growth and development, as well as to a better distribution of the benefits of that growth within the community.

In the words of Herman E.Daly, « *It is hard to imagine how any thorough transformation of the habits of humans will occur without a corporate human confidence in the ultimate worthwhileness of our moral endeavors* ». Conscious development expresses, in its conception, the limits of economic growth and development in their current forms, since resources are limited and also because of the risks at the level of human and ecological potential. Conscious development cannot simply be a continuous adaptation of an economic system: it must also meet the needs, that is to say, restore the balance between growth, resources and environment, promote a better distribution of growth benefits through moral values as the spirit of fairness, justice, etc.; reduce the consequences of economic growth on the environment and contribute to improving the quality of life communities in a sustainable time perspective. Conscious development encompasses all the factors of economic growth, since the latter includes especially the factor of "conscience." If progress is measured by the achievement of the

---

[55]   E. E. HAGEN, op.,cit., p. 107.

purposes, growth and development efforts are measured by goals that must be maintained at the level of basic development factors (growth), namely education, infrastructure and health.

2. <u>AWARENESS AS A FACTOR OF DEVELOPMENT</u>

The issues raised in our state-of-the matter requires an awareness of all the communities at local, regional, national as well as at the subnational level. These problems require at the level of different communities, an individual awareness, on the one hand, and collective, on the other. There is a reciprocal relationship between individual consciousness and collective consciousness. This means that each individual within the community influences the collective conscience of the community, and, conversely, each person is influenced by the collective consciousness. It is obvious that the collective consciousness of a community both locally and within the country can be improved through the development of individual consciousness. According to Maharishi, the fundamental force that governs the quality of social life is the collective consciousness of society. The collective consciousness of a group represents the entire consciousness of this group.

Each level of the society has its own collective consciousness, hence people speak to the family, community, region, country consciousness. In the country, the conscience of the individual determines the quality of his thoughts and behavior. Similarly, there is a quality of consciousness for each social group (family, region, country) with its own reality and its possibilities for development. The quality of the collective consciousness of a social group is a direct and true reflection of the level of consciousness of its members. As everyone knows, every family has a specific feature. This is the same for behavior patterns and cultural values of each geographic location that are distinct even at the national level. The quality of the collective consciousness of each unit (individual) contributes to the quality of consciousness of a wider social group. Thus, the quality of the collective consciousness of each province affects the quality of national consciousness[56]. Conscious development is primarily a conscious process of imagination characterized by conscious acts in response to various community problems through educational action according to a "social" logic. Indeed, it is not possible to improve or plan a development model that is identical to all communities even they are from the same country or region. Given that development is a "social" logic, the search of objective, that is, the best living conditions of individuals, is a concept that varies from one society to another and from one community to another. Every society or community will define its quality of life according to its priority or priorities. It is unrealistic that everyone adopts the same lifestyle. Thus, the search for the quality of life does not necessarily mean the quantity of goods, although a minimum of consumption is required to meet basic needs. It is true that development does not always bring happiness as outlined by Hill McKibben: « *Growth is no longer making most people wealthier, but instead generating inequality and insecurity . . . Research from many quarters has started to show that even growth does make us wealthier, the greater wealth no longer makes us happier* »[57]. Hence development activities should contribute mainly to improving the quality of life of communities for which and through they are undertaken, this is what justifies the choice of conscious development to meet this objective. To access a better quality of life, the development concrete action to be undertaken must be conscious.

---

56   M. MAHESH Yogi, ibid., p.122.

57   B. McKIBBEN , Deep Economy. The Wealth of Communities and the Durable Future. Ed.Times books, New York, 2007, p.1.

Conscious development is the result of the realization of a set of acts carried out consciously by the community thanks to the goals of education in general, and of environmental and traditional education, in particular. Our belief is that development should or should always be a conscious process through the community education. Educational action is therefore the basis of the process of conscious development. Conscious development is also characterized by a willful and conscious acceptance or refusal, by a given community, of a development model (project action, investment) because the latter meets or does not meet the ethical and moral goal as well the development goals internalized by the population through education. It is not enough to become aware of a fact, but it is important to translate this awareness into action. As Mao Zedong, quoted by Daniel Altman, said « *If you want to know the theory and methods of revolution, you must take part in revolution* »[58]. Conscious development is pragmatic. Many problems concerning the development of our communities, countries or regions, for example, are clearly identified and solutions are also known. But there has never been this conscious commitment on behalf of ones or the others (political leaders, communities . . .) to translate these solutions into action although all the conditions of their realization or materialization are known and met. Unfortunately, as Herbert Agar, says « *The truth that makes men free is for the most part the truth which men prefer not to hear* »[59]. Thus, for example, to leave to our future generations a better environment, as advocated by the concept of sustainable development, men should translate into action their awareness. Thus it can be stated that development can not only be endogenous, integrated or sustainable, it must above all be conscious. It's when communities have materialized

[58]   Mao Zedong cité par D. ALTMAN, Neoconomy, op.cit., p.71.

[59]   H. AGAR cité par D. ICKE, op.cit., p.147.

this awareness into action that they will really take care of themselves instead of undergoing what they are being forced to accept which is against their will, against their development and their environment. It is urgent for each individual to be aware of his responsibilities vis-à-vis the community and the environment. The effects of any decision should be viewed not only in relation to technical, commercial or financial data, but also in terms of moral and ethical issues that we seek to achieve and to promote within the community.

Consciousness must help critically evaluate the development actions being considered to be undertaken and to evaluate them according to a system of moral, spiritual and cultural characteristics of each community[60]. Thus, not any model of development is appropriate, likewise not any science application is acceptable.

3.2.9. <u>FROM CONCEPTION TO ACTION</u>

As noted below, conscious development must be translated into daily actions. However, it is up to communities themselves to determine the most appropriate and adequate means to promote their development and that, taking into account the realities on the ground, local, regional or national priorities, etc . . . Kevin Danacher et al.,assert « *To create a globally sustainable economy, we must have local networks exerting effective control over local conditions. Sometimes this local control will have an obvious green element and sometimes it will not* »[61]. There is no universal formula, simple or identical to all communities to undertake action. Needs will be dictated and decisions will be made depending on the socio-economic, political, institutional, structural and cultural context

---

[60] M. MALDAGUE, op.cit., p.61.

[61] K. DANACHER, S. BIGGS and J. MARK, op. cit., p.112.

of each community. However, priorities will be established according to resources. For George S.Clason, « *where the determination is, the way can be found* »[62]. Conscious development is a process of conscious imagination, thus each community is or will find answers to issues that hinder its development. In response to the problem of urban transport in Kisangani, for example, the community introduced the bicycle transportation system "Toleka", in Kinshasa, buses called "Fula-Fula" used to transport people, a system that has now disappeared, then came the "taxi-bus" and now "motorbike are used as taxis." In response to the problem of organizing funerals in their compounds, Kinshasa people today use a system of funeral service which consisting in renting tents, catafalque, in public places spreading. To meet the security needs of the city, the police adopted the system of spreading sub-stations through the different areas of the city and installed 40' containers which serve as Police offices. In the next part of this section, we will focus on two important aspects of conscious development, namely the nature of conscious development activities and its implementation.

1. NATURE OF CONSCIOUS DEVELOPMENT ACTIVITIES

We witness, as usual, a predominance of material progress on development goals to be achieved. About material progress, TH Monod wrote, «*We are witnesses today of a very' strange phenomenon with major potential concern's that is, we, at last, do things, not because we have taken time to think on them and have finally concluded they are useful to progress, but only because we have the material means of doing them. Is*

---

[62] G. S. CLASON, The Richestman in Babylon. The Success Secrets of the Ancients, Ed.Aplume book, New York, 2005, p.116.

this a reasonable justification for a sensible person as the homo sapiens»[63]
(« *On assiste à un phénomène singulier aux conséquences potentielles très préoccupantes, c'est que l'on finit par faire les choses, non pas parce qu'on y a réfléchi longuement et qu'on a fini par constater qu'elles étaient utiles au progrès, mais parce qu'on peut matériellement les faire. Est-ce là une justification raisonnable pour un être pensant comme homo sapiens?* »). It is therefore necessary to distinguish between positive conscious activities and negative conscious activities. As J.Fletcher said «*The morality of an act is a function of the state of the system at the time it is performed* »[64]. An economic or non-economic is said to be conscious and positive when it is positive to the needs of the community who undertakes it or wants to undertake it because it meets its welfare objectives. An economic or non-economic is said conscious and negative when it is characterized by a negative result and does not meet the development goals (welfare) of the community, this is the case, for example, of the practice of cutting fruit trees to get charcoal in rural area of DRCongo. Positive or negative conscious activities are not only economic. They also display different socio-cultural, political, moral, institutional aspect of the communities. On this aspect Monod said, «*if ignorance is serious, it is, however, less serious than the deficiency in terms of reflective consciousness. Because technologican compensate more and more our intellectual weakness and our reduced capacity of data processing, but will be of no help regarding the inability of so many managers to filter their decisions through conscious reflection*»[65] (« *si l'ignorance est grave, elle l'est moins cependant que la*

---

[63] TH. MONOD, « Qui règnera demain ? La qualité ou la quantité ?» dans Comptes rendus du 1er colloque international sur l'Environnement, UNESCO, CNB/FUL Arlon/Belgique, Cahier n°1, p.106.

[64] J. FLETCHER cité par D. KENNEDY, State of the Planet 2006-2007, IslandPress, Washington DC, 2006, p.120.

[65] TH. MONOD, op.cit., p.106.

carence sur le plan de la conscience réfléchie. Car la technique pourra compenser de plus en plus notre faiblesse intellectuelle et notre capacité réduite de traitement des données, mais ne sera d'aucun secours en ce qui concerne l'inaptitude de tant de responsables de passer leurs décisions au crible d'une réflexion consciente »).

Breaking the deadlock involves a new mindset on behalf of decision makers, both politicians as well as other development actors in the world. In short, «*a revolution of conscious is as fundamental as were the scientific and industrial revolutions*»[66] (« *une révolution de la conscience est aussi fondamentale que l'ont été les révolutions scientifiques et industrielles* »). Moreover, Michel Maldague, writes «*it is ironic that in the late twentieth century where information continues to grow and where the technological means to inform refinements have reached extraordinary ignorance and lack of reflective consciousness is widespread . . . Reflective consciousness must be involved in other elements which affect the progress of man as far as one wishes to maintain the balance between man and the biosphere*» (« *il est paradoxal de constater qu'en cette fin de siècle où l'information ne cesse de se multiplier et où les moyens technologiques de s'informer ont atteint des perfectionnements extraordinaires, l'ignorance et l'absence de conscience réfléchie sont très largement répandues . . . La conscience réfléchie doit intervenir dans les autres éléments qui conditionnent le progrès de l'homme pour autant qu'on désire maintenir l'équilibre entre l'homme et la biosphère* »). As for as we are concerned, the purpose and goal of education should lead to an awareness of communities and an increasing awareness in the development. This awareness has a mental origin, that is to say, in the minds of people and must be translated into concrete acts, physical, social, moral, cultural and intellectual acts that the population wants to achieve. It is this second

---

[66]   TH. MONOD, op.cit., p.106.

phase (materialization) that characterizes conscious development. All development activities to be undertaken in one country may or may not be beneficial to the development of our communities. This is the case of some activities undertaken because of an unconscious and sometimes immoral exploitation of resources for a pseudo-development. This form of unconscious and uncontrolled development is characterized by the acceptance of any type of investment or project to be implemented in the country, some of them are fallacious such as the import of toxic waste, as this was the case a few years ago in some African countries for some money. The experience in our country has shown that for the sake of development, we accepted any investment under conditions which are sometimes irresponsible to the expense of our communities.

This is the case, for example, the rise of bakery industries of which the monthly and annual imports of wheat cost a fortune to the country in the terms of currencies. It is shown that if one tenth of the amount spent on the import of corn were devoted to the development of cassava and other local products (and even the production of wheat, as has been attempted by MIDEMA Kivu) the country and the population would the great beneficiaries. Instead, we fund investments that alter the eating habits of the population. It is important to remember that chikwangue and "fufu" were used during breakfast before going to school or work, which used to give a lot of work to peasants who had to produce more and more, and allowed the country to save enough currencies necessary for the development of other sectors (education, infrastructure, health, . . .). This unconsciousness can be illustrated by other examples. The case of the massive import of mackerel at the expense of development of the local fishing industry. The amount of money spent on imports would develop this promising local industry. The same situation applied to Livestock Development. In short, it is by this change of mentality and this awareness by the combined action of environmental and traditional education that we will be able to accept what is good and reject what is bad for our development and our environment according the interest expressed by the communities, because, indeed, it is harmful to go against their deep will. This awareness must be manifested in our institutions and leaders toward our communities. For example, the determination of the population of Kinshasa to counter the rebels in August 1998 is a real evidence of consciousness expressed by this population to ensure peace and security. Another example that can help us is the refusal by the kasaïen people to the bank notes (called prostate) issued from a monetary reform led by these former Prime Minister Birindwa. Beyond all speculations, the kasaïen people survived despite their refusal to use these bank notes which would have affected their socio-economic development. This example should help communities across the country. They have to promote their development by rejecting development actions which are contrary to the objectives and ethics of true and sustainable development. It is important to consider the adverse effects that may because by development projects on resources, environment and community development. It is worth reporting the example of Americans consciences who think that: « *A third of American consumers said that the primary goal of business should be building a better society—and are willing to support those that do so, seizing the chance to make a positive contribution through their purchasing decision* »[67].

---

[67] H. NOREENA, Global Capitalism and the Death of Democracy. Ed.harperBusiness, New York, p.202, 2003.

Bibliography

1. **ALTMAN D.** : Neoconomy. George Bush's revolutionary gamble with america's future, Ed. PublicAffairs, New york, 2004.

2. **BERNA M. and TORR J.D.** : Developping Nations, Greenhaven press, New York, 2003.

3. **BERNA M. and TORR J.D.** : Developping Nations, Greenhaven press, New York, 2003.

4. **COHEN D.S.** : The heart of change. Field grade. Tools and tactics for leading change in your organization, Harvard Business School press, Boston/Massachusset, 2005.

5. **CLASON G.S.** : The richestman in Babylon. The success secrets of the Ancients. Ed. Aplumebokk, New york, 2005.

6. **EDWENE G.** : Four spiritual laws of prosperity, Ed. Rodale, USA, 2005.

7. **ERVIN L. et SEIDEL P.** : Global Survival, Selectbooks inc, New York, 2006.

    LARRY B. and RAM C. : Execution. The discipline of getting things done, Crown business, New York, 2002.

8. **MCKIBBEN B.** : Deep Economy. The wealth of communities and the durable future. Ed. Times Book, New york, 2007.

9. **MAHARISHI MAHESH YOGI** : Creating an ideal society. Rheinweiler, West Germany, MERU Press, 1977.

10. **MAHARISHI MAHESH YOGI** : Life supported by natural law, Age of Enlightenment Press, Washington DC, 1986.

11. **MALDAGUE M.** : Etapes du développement technologique et évolution de la société, dans Problématique de la crise de l'environnement, 3°édition, Un. Laval, 1980

12. **MALDAGUE M.** : Gestion de l'Environnement Tropical, Vol.I, Université de Laval, Canada, 1988.

13. **MICHAEL J. M.** : Rational exuberance. Silencing the enemies of growth and why the future is better than you think; HarperBusiness, New York, 2004.

14. **MICKLETHWAIT J. et WOOLDRIDGE A.** : A future perfect. The challenge and hidden promise of globalization, Ed. Crown business, New York, 2000.

15. **MILTON F.** : Capitalism and freedom, Ed. The university of Chicago press, Chicago, 2002.

16. **MONOD TH.** : Qui règnera demain?, La quantité ou la qualité"?, dans Comptes rendus du premier colloque international sur l'environnement, Unesco, septembre 1979, cahier n°1, Paris, 1980.

17. **MUHAMMAD Y.** : Banker to the poor. Micro-lending and the battle against world poverty, PublicAffairs, New York, 2003.

18. **NOREENA H.** : Global Capitalism and the death of democracy. The silent takeover, Harperbusiness, New York, 2003.

19.	ORMEROD P.	:	Why most things fail ? Evolution, Extinction and Economics ; Wiley&sons, New York, 2005.
20.	O'ROURKE P.J.	:	The wealth of nations, Grove press, New york, 2006.
21.	SACHS J.D.	:	The end of poverty, Ed. The penguin press, New York, 2005.
22.	SHAPIRO T.M.	:	The hidden cost of being african american. How wealth perpetuates inequality, Ed. Oxford Press university, New York, 2004.
23.	STEPHEN C. S.	:	Ending Global Poverty, Palgrave Macmillan, New York, 2005.
24.	STEVEN D. L. et STEPHEN J.D.	:	Freakonomics. A rogue economist express the hidden sick of everything, Harper Collins, New York, 2005.
25.	STEVEN E. L.	:	More sex is safer sex. The unconventional wisdom of economics, Free press, New York, 2007.
26.	SUDHIR A. VENKATESH A.	:	Off the books. The underground economy of the urban poor, Harvard University Press, Massachussetts, 2006.
27.	VAN PARYS J.M.	:	Petite introduction à l'éthique, Ed. Loyola, Kinshasa, 1993.
28.	WADE L.	:	The ten commandments, Ed. Gerald Wheeler, USA, 2006.
29.	WARSH D.	:	Knowledge and the wealth of nations. A story of economic discovery, Ed. W.W. Norton & Co, New York, 2006.

30. **WOLFENSOHN J.D.** : Les défis de la mondialisation. Le rôle de la banque Mondiale, Banque Mondiale, Washington DC, 2001.

31. **WWF** : Living Planet Report 2012, www.wwf.org

PUBLICATIONS

1. Le développement conscient. Un autre regard de développement, Ed. AuthorHouse, IL, USA, 2012.
2. Le modèle monade de développement. Le développement des communautés en Afrique, Ed.AuthorHouse, IL, USA, 2012.
3. Comment sortir de l'impasse du sous-développement en Afrique. Diversité des communautés et diversité des solutions, Ed.Universitaires Européennes, Sarrebruck, Allemagne, 2012.
4. Etude économique et développement de la région Nekongo en RDC, Ed.Authorhouse, Il, USA, 2014.
5. Conscious development. Another Approach to Sustainable development, Ed.Authorhouse, IL, USA, 2014.